STARSEEKER

Phil Porter

STARSEEKER

Based on the novel by Tim Bowler

OBERON BOOKS
LONDON

WWW.OBERONBOOKS.COM

First published in this adaptation in 2007 by Oberon Books Ltd
521 Caledonian Road, London N7 9RH
Tel: +44 (0) 20 7607 3637 / Fax: +44 (0) 20 7607 3629
e-mail: info@oberonbooks.com
www.oberonbooks.com

A catalogue record for this book is available from the British
Library.

PB ISBN: 978-1-84002-793-8

Visit www.oberonbooks.com to read more about all our books and to buy
them. You will also find features, author interviews and news of any author
events, and you can sign up for e-newsletters so that you're always first to
hear about our new releases.

Characters

LUKE

MRS LITTLE

SKIN

DAZ

MIRANDA

MUM

ROGER

MR HARDING

NATALIE / BARLEY

DAD

DANIEL

SQUADRON LEADER HUTCHINSON

MRS ROBERTS

MR ROBERTS

Punctuation

/ = speech is interrupted

… = speech trails off

This stage adaptation of *Starseeker* was first performed at Theatre Royal, Northampton, on 22 June 2007, with the following cast:

LUKE, Michael George Moore

SKIN / DAD / MR HARDING, Ryan Early

DAZ / ROGER / MR ROBERTS, James Thorne

MUM / MRS LITTLE / MRS ROBERTS, Eve Dallas

MIRANDA / NATALIE, Tamsin Fessey

Director, Dani Parr

Designer, Kate Bunce

Sound Designer, Gareth Fry

Lighting Designer, Malcolm Rippeth

SEQUENCE ONE

LUKE stands alone in a pool of light. A persistent but shifting humming sound envelopes him.

LUKE: Sometimes, I hear a sound.
    I hear a lot of sounds,
    But sometimes…
    Like a humming sound.
    Like machinery in a basement.
    Or sometimes like a roar.
    Or sometimes just a murmur,
    Like the water on the weir.

He presses a finger against the side of his head. The sound and light become euphoric as LUKE gets lost in his fantasy…

    And sometimes,
    When I close my eyes,
    I feel like I'm flying.
    Surrounded by trees,
    I'm going up past the branches,
    Through the leaves,
    Like I'm lighter than air.
    And it's a daytime sky,
    But with flashes of gold,
    And above me there's a bright speck of light.
    And next to me… Dad.
    And we fly towards the light
    Until it's all we can see,
    Until the world is nothing
    But light.

*

A grey light picks out MRS LITTLE, an old and peculiar-looking woman, standing by a high window, looking out. She is holding a box. The box has a black velvet exterior, thick silver beading on its lid and a brocade tassel. From somewhere behind MRS LITTLE comes the sound of a girl crying. The sound is not piercing or harrowing, just a sad and steady, heartfelt cry.

Cradling the box with great tenderness, MRS LITTLE lifts its lid and looks inside. She has seen its contents many times before. To look at them brings both pain and relief. The light on MRS LITTLE becomes hotter and the girl's cry becomes just slightly more urgent. MRS LITTLE closes her eyes for a moment. She opens her eyes and closes the box gently. The light and the crying fade away.

*

LUKE stands at the bottom of a drainpipe that runs down the side of MRS LITTLE's house. He takes hold of the drainpipe and looks up, planning his climb. SKIN and DAZ are with him...

SKIN: So. We want you to be part of the gang. But we need to know we can trust you.

DAZ: We need to know you've got the bottle.

SKIN: You're either for us or against us, Luke. That's the way it is. And you don't want to be against us, if you get my meaning.

LUKE begins to climb the drainpipe. He is a skilled climber.

That's it. Good boy.

DAZ: Good boy, Luke.

SKIN: You know what to do. If you see the box, you grab it. It's black velvet and silver /

DAZ: Obsessed with that box, you are, Skin /

SKIN: Shut up, Daz. If not, you come down to the front door and you let us in.

DAZ: Yeah, leave it to the professionals.

SKIN: You got that?

DAZ: You got that, Lukey Boy?!

The sound of the girl crying comes back. It has a peculiar, unreal quality to it. LUKE stops climbing.

SKIN: Don't stop, what have you stopped for? She'll be back soon. (*Pause.*) Oi!

The sound of crying remains but LUKE resumes his climb.

That's more like it. Now get in.

LUKE clambers through a window and closes it behind him. He finds himself at the top of a staircase on a small landing area. There are two closed doors in front of him and a staircase leading down. The sound of the crying girl remains. It feels much closer now. He tentatively approaches a door. He puts his ear to the door and for a brief moment the sound feels closer still. The sound stops abruptly. An eerie silence.

LUKE: (*Whispers.*) I won't hurt you. I promise. I promise I won't hurt you.

LUKE nervously puts a hand on the doorknob. He twists and pushes but the door is locked. He kneels down and looks through a keyhole. He sees a bedroom – a bed, a radiator, faded wallpaper, empty shelves – dimly lit by the last of the day's light through a skylight. Suddenly, NATALIE's face appears at the keyhole, her eyes wet with tears. She stares at LUKE. He draws back from the door, frightened. She begins to cry again as he runs down the stairs.

*

LUKE is now climbing a large oak tree. He climbs with great skill and knows every branch, knot and crevice. He reaches a tree-house and climbs in, out of sight. Seconds later, SKIN and DAZ arrive at the bottom of the tree, out of breath from running. They take a moment to catch their breath and spit. They speak quietly to one another...

DAZ: Reckon he's up there?

SKIN: Course he is.

They call out to LUKE...

(*Friendly.*) Luke? Luke, you up there, mate?

DAZ: We know you're up there, we can see you.

SKIN: Chuck the rope ladder down, will you, mate?

DAZ: Yeah, chuck the rope ladder down.

They speak quietly to one another...

We could try and climb it.

SKIN: Yeah, we tried that before remember. Nearly broke my neck. Come on, let's go, he's got to face us soon enough. (*Calls out.*) You got to face us soon enough, Lukey Boy!

DAZ: Yeah! You can't stay in your special little tree forever, Lukey Boy!

SKIN: Shut up, Daz.

SKIN and DAZ go. LUKE peers out of the tree-house to check they have gone. He sits in the tree-house looking out across the forest and up at the night sky. He hears NATALIE crying. He holds onto a branch, gripping it for comfort. The sound subsides. He climbs down from the tree-house silently. He stands at the foot of the tree and speaks to it...

LUKE: 'Night.

As LUKE walks away, SKIN appears in front of him. LUKE stops.

SKIN: Little bastard.

LUKE: All right, Skin?

LUKE thinks about making a run for it but DAZ is behind him.

DAZ: Chicken bastard.

SKIN: All you had to do was leave the front door open. That was you done. Now we've got to wait 'til she goes out again, all cos you got freaked out by an empty house.

LUKE: It wasn't empty.

DAZ: Course it was.

SKIN: Well, we're breaking into that place and you're going to help.

DAZ: Whether you like it or not.

SKIN: We're meeting tomorrow morning, eight o'clock, top of the track, we'll make a new plan, you got that?

LUKE: All right. (*Pause.*) Can I go now?

Pause.

SKIN: Yeah, course.

Pause. LUKE starts to walk away but SKIN grabs him by the throat.

Just as soon as I've taught you a lesson in respect.

*

MIRANDA plays her flute without accompaniment – The Dance of the Blessed Spirits by Gluck. After a few bars she stops and goes back over a phrase. She goes over the phrase twice more, slowing it down, getting it right.

SEQUENCE TWO

MUM and ROGER are standing outside the front door of LUKE's house. They stand close together, holding one another's hands.

MUM: Thanks, Roger.

ROGER: What for?

MUM: For understanding. With Luke. It's difficult.

ROGER: I know.

Pause.

MUM: He's just hurting at the moment.

ROGER: You don't have to explain, honestly, I understand. (*Pause.*) I'd better go.

11

MUM: All right. Take care.

ROGER: And you.

> *After a pause, they kiss. After the kiss, they hold each other for a couple of seconds. As they are doing this, LUKE arrives, unnoticed by MUM and ROGER. His face is cut and swollen. He watches them. MUM goes back into the house. ROGER turns and sees LUKE.*

> Luke. (*Pause. He feels caught out. He notices LUKE's injuries.*) Are you all right?

LUKE: Why shouldn't I be?

ROGER: Your face.

LUKE: What about it?

> *Pause.*

ROGER: You're late back, your mum was worried.

LUKE: Didn't seem it just now.

ROGER: Well, she was. (*Pause.*) Luke, I'd like to be able to talk to you. About stuff, about me and your mum, about everything. But, at the moment, I can't. Because I'm nervous /

LUKE: Nervous of what?

ROGER: Of you, I /

LUKE: What, and that's my fault, is it?

ROGER: No.

LUKE: Can't help it if you feel nervous, can I? I can't help the way you feel.

ROGER: I know that.

LUKE: Don't blame me.

ROGER: I don't blame you. I don't blame you for anything. I just wish /

LUKE: Yeah, whatever.

LUKE pushes past ROGER.

ROGER: Luke.

LUKE walks into the house.

Night, Luke.

ROGER heads home.

*

MIRANDA practises the flute. Starting with the phrase she stopped on last time, she plays more of The Dance of the Blessed Spirits.

*

LUKE is sitting on his bed. His mum is cleaning his face. She has cotton wool and a bowl of disinfected water.

MUM: What's happening to you? (*Pause.*) You hang around with those horrible boys, come back late every night. If I ask a question you bite my head off. You've stopped trying at school /

LUKE: I try in music.

MUM: Not like you used to. Luke, you've got a gift, but if you neglect that gift, it'll disappear.

LUKE: I'm not neglecting anything.

MUM: You are, you've stopped performing, you hardly do any practice.

LUKE: The stuff they give me's boring, it's too easy. And who says I've stopped performing? I've told Mr Harding I'll play in the concert.

MUM: Well, I'm glad about that.

LUKE: Yeah, so what's the problem?!

He pushes her hand away from his face. She has finished cleaning him anyway, so she hands him an ice pack to hold against his bruised eyes.

MUM: Sooner or later /

LUKE: Sooner or later what?

MUM: Sooner or later, you're going to have to talk to me.

LUKE: What are we doing now?

MUM: About Dad.

LUKE: Yeah, I don't want to. I already told you that. You said I didn't have to, not if I didn't want to.

MUM: That was two years ago. If you keep bottling it up, we'll never get through this.

LUKE will not look at her.

What, you think you're the only one that got hurt?

He still will not look at her.

It's difficult for me too, you know.

LUKE shakes his head.

What? If you've got something to say, why don't you say it?

LUKE: It didn't look too difficult on the porch just now. (*Pause.*) He's asked you to marry him, hasn't he? (*Pause.*) And what did you say?

MUM: I said I'd think about it.

The sound of NATALIE crying comes back, quietly at first...

LUKE: What's there to think about? You're going to say yes.

MUM: Would you hate it if I did?

LUKE: Well, it's nothing to do with me, is it?

MUM: Of course it is. Luke, you're all I've got.

LUKE: No I'm not, you've got Mr Gillmore.

MUM: For God's sake, his name's Roger, call him Roger! Why don't you like him? Is it because you think he's going to take me away from you? Or is it just because he isn't Dad?

The crying is very loud now. LUKE is clutching his head.

What's the matter?

LUKE: Nothing is /

MUM: Luke?

LUKE: Nothing!

The sound goes. Silence.

I just can't deal with this whole marriage thing right now, okay? Got too much on my mind.

MUM: Okay. (*Pause.*) I understand that. (*Pause.*) I love you.

MUM waits for a response but doesn't get one. She goes. LUKE stands, closes his eyes and takes deep breaths. The euphoric sound and light of LUKE's flying fantasy come back.

SEQUENCE THREE

LUKE is lying on the grass by a brook. A bridge passes over the brook just behind LUKE. It is morning and the sun is shining. LUKE is asleep. SKIN and DAZ appear on the bridge above him. They stand over him for a moment but he doesn't wake up...

SKIN: So, what are you doing here, Luke?

LUKE wakes up. SKIN and DAZ join LUKE on the ground...

LUKE: All right, Skin.

SKIN: I thought we were meeting at The Grange. Thought we had an agreement.

LUKE: I was about to go.

SKIN: Yeah, you were meant to be there half an hour ago.

LUKE: I didn't know what time.

SKIN: You deaf? I said eight.

DAZ: Eight o'clock.

LUKE: I thought you said half past.

SKIN: (*Grabbing LUKE's throat.*) Don't muck me about, Luke. I don't like it when people muck me about, you know that. Why do you muck me about like this?

DAZ: He reckons he's too good for us, that's why.

SKIN: Is that it? Do you reckon you're too good for us?

DAZ: Cos he plays the piano.

SKIN: Is that what it is?

LUKE: No /

SKIN: Does mummy not want you hanging round with us?

LUKE: None of her business who I hang round with.

SKIN: (*Lets go of LUKE's throat with a push.*) Right. So we'll see you at midnight. Just up from The Grange. You can make up for last time.

LUKE: What, break in again?

DAZ: He's quick, ain't he? You're quick.

LUKE: Tonight?

SKIN: I just said so, didn't I?

LUKE: But she'll be in the house. I thought that was the point, do it on a Friday evening when she's at the shop. She'll hear me.

SKIN: At midnight? She'll be asleep.

LUKE: Yeah, what if she wakes up though?

SKIN: Then you run away, don't you?

DAZ: Yeah, you're good at running away, ain't you, Lukey?

LUKE: Come on, Skin, I'd get done by the police. Why's it got to be me?

SKIN: What's the matter with you? You should be pleased we want you in the gang. And you know why it's got to be you. Cos you're the best at climbing, ain't you, Monkey Boy? And cos you know your way round the house now, don't you, after your last little visit? And because you owe me for messing it up last time, all right? You owe me big time, Luke Stanton.

MIRANDA appears.

MIRANDA: Luke?

SKIN: Oh, hello, Miranda.

DAZ: Hello, Miranda.

MIRANDA: Hi. Luke /

SKIN: How are you?

MIRANDA: Fine, thank you /

SKIN: Still riding?

DAZ sniggers.

MIRANDA: Pardon?

SKIN: Still riding that horse? Only I haven't seen you go past my house lately. Used to really like that, I did, watching

17

you come past. (*He leers at* MIRANDA.) So, what can we do for you, beautiful?

MIRANDA: Nothing. I want to speak to Luke.

SKIN: Oh, I'm sorry, you should have said. How very rude of us. Come on, Daz, let's leave them to it, shall we? Don't want to stand in the way of true love. We're all sorted here anyway, ain't we, Lukey?

LUKE: Yeah.

SKIN: Good. I'm pleased. Later then.

DAZ: Yeah, later, Lukey.

SKIN and DAZ go. Pause.

MIRANDA: What happened to your face?

LUKE: Nothing.

MIRANDA: Were you in a fight or something?

LUKE: It doesn't matter.

MIRANDA: Did they do it? (*Pause.*) Why do you hang round with them, Luke? It doesn't make any sense. They're horrible. And they stink /

LUKE: Just leave it, I said it's not a problem. (*Pause.*) What did you want?

MIRANDA: Oh. It's nothing really /

LUKE: Okay, well, I'd better go, so /

MIRANDA: No, hang on, don't go. I mean, it's not nothing, there is something. Can you help me with something?

LUKE: What?

MIRANDA: Well, I told Mr Harding I'd do a flute piece at the concert. But the thing is, I need someone to do the piano part.

LUKE: Yeah, sorry, I'm already doing a piece.

MIRANDA: I know that, but... I mean, you're so good and everything, I thought maybe you could do both.

LUKE: Can't Melanie do it?

MIRANDA: Yeah, if you don't want to. It's just she's a bit, you know... (*She does an impression of Melanie's piano playing.*) I just thought... Because I'm not much good, so I thought if you played, because you're so good, I thought it might cover up my mistakes. But if you don't want to /

LUKE: Okay.

MIRANDA: What, you'll do it?

LUKE: Why not?

MIRANDA: Really?

LUKE: Course.

MIRANDA: That's brilliant. It's called The Dance of the Blessed Spirits.

LUKE: No problem.

MIRANDA: Thanks. Honestly, I've been getting in such a state. So, if I give you a ring later, could we sort out a practice session?

LUKE: If you like.

MIRANDA: That would be great, thanks so much. (*Pause.*) See, it's not that hard, is it?

LUKE: What?

MIRANDA: To be the real you. Instead of all this other stuff.

LUKE smiles. MIRANDA goes. The soundscape begins to alter. At first, it is just a subtle change in the 'real' sounds that surround LUKE. The birdsong and the sound of the brook take on a peculiar, invasive quality. But soon they give way to a sound that

19

is familiar from the beginning of Sequence One – a persistent, vibrating hum. After a time, that sound builds and deepens to become a roar, both menacing and appealing…

LUKE: That sound again.
That humming sound.
Only stronger now.
Like a rumble this time.
Like thunder this time.
Like a wave getting closer.
Like a tidal wave
But all around.

The sound of a piano emerges from within the roar: Tchaikovsy's Douce Reverie.

Then piano music.
Childish…
Child music.
It's beautiful.
I know this music.
What is it?

All sound but the piano music fades away. The music leads us into…

SEQUENCE FOUR

LUKE is standing in the middle of MR HARDING's teaching room. MR HARDING is sitting in a chair. There is a piano. LUKE is lost in Douce Reverie.

HARDING: Come and sit down.

LUKE does not hear MR HARDING, only the music.

Luke?

LUKE: (*To himself.*) What is it?

The music fades away. LUKE turns to look at MR HARDING.

HARDING: Come and sit down.

LUKE: Don't you want me to play?

HARDING: Not just now.

LUKE sits with MR HARDING. MR HARDING stares at LUKE. The sound of a bouncing ball invades LUKE's head.

We'll make this lesson a freebie. Since we're just sitting around.

The ball bounces some more and a child laughs.

What are you hearing, Luke?

A mysterious cacophony erupts: the bouncing ball, the laughing child, the mad scuttling of insects, that familiar humming sound. He presses a finger against the side of his head. The other sounds die out, leaving only the humming sound. A few notes from Douce Reverie are heard over the hum before LUKE's head becomes quiet again.

'The isle is full of noises.'

LUKE: What's that supposed to mean?

HARDING: It's a quotation. (*Pause.*) Do you know what I see when I look at you? I see a person made of music. I see a person consumed by music. I see a person with the capacity to experience music and sound and life in a way that's beyond even the imagination of ordinary people like me. What an amazing thing, Luke! What a gift! (*Pause.*) What I'm saying, if life's getting difficult, let your gift guide you. Let it help you /

LUKE: I don't need any help.

HARDING: Well I think you do. I think you're at war.

LUKE: Who with?

HARDING: Everyone. Especially yourself.

LUKE: I don't need this.

HARDING: Look at you.

LUKE: I don't need this!

HARDING: Okay.

LUKE: Why can't people leave me alone?!

HARDING: All right, Luke, I'm sorry. I'm worried about you, that's all. A lot of people are.

Pause. Six notes from Douce Reverie.

LUKE: Mr Harding?

HARDING: Yes?

LUKE: Have you got the sheet music for Scenes From Childhood?

HARDING: No, I lent it to someone. Why?

LUKE: Or The Children's Corner Suite?

HARDING: I thought you didn't like Debussy. (*Pause.*) Is this for the concert?

LUKE: No, something else.

Intrigued, MR HARDING begins a search for The Children's Corner Suite.

Anyway, I thought you wanted me to play that other piece for the concert.

HARDING: I've been thinking about that. Why don't you play something different? It's your last concert and it's my last concert, play something you really want to play. (*He finds The Children's Corner Suite.*) The Children's Corner Suite by Claude Debussy.

LUKE takes the music from MR HARDING and rifles through it in search of the childlike tune in his head…

In fact, don't even tell me what you're going to play. Surprise me. Play something that means something to you. (*He sees that LUKE is hardly listening.*) Got what you wanted?

LUKE: Not really.

HARDING: The Snow Is Dancing, that's a nice piece. Play it for me.

LUKE sits at the piano and plays...

'The isle is full of noises.'

LUKE continues to play, leading us into...

SEQUENCE FIVE

A laptop computer glows invitingly on a desk in a dark room. LUKE sits at the desk to check his email account. He clicks the mouse twice and then types. He speaks the words that he types...

LUKE: Username lukestanton92. Password peanut. (*Click.*) Inbox. Jason Skinner. (*Click. SKIN appears.*)

SKIN: Midnight. Or else.

Pause.

LUKE: (*Click. SKIN disappears.*) Inbox. Miranda Davis. (*Click. MIRANDA appears.*)

MIRANDA: Hi Luke. Thanks so much for saying you'll help me with my piece. Now the piano bit will be good, even if the flute bits are rubbish. I tried it with Melanie, which was okay, but she fidgets and sniffs a lot, which puts me off. Are you free tomorrow at eleven to practise? You could come to mine and use our piano or I could come to you. Thanks again, this means such a lot to me. Love, Miranda. Smiley face, kiss kiss. Kiss.

LUKE: Reply. (*Click. He types...*) Tomorrow at eleven is fine. See you at yours. Luke. Send. (*Click. MIRANDA disappears.*)

LUKE sits back in his chair. His head fills with the humming sound, which morphs into the sound of an aeroplane overhead. Silence.

Log out. (*Click.*) Log in. (*Click.*) Username kirstistanton.
Password edvardgrieg. (*Click.*) Inbox. Roger Gillmore.
(*Pause. Click. ROGER appears.*)

ROGER: Kirsti, I'll wait forever if that's what it takes. All my
love, Roger.

*Pause. LUKE thumps the desk. Pause. LUKE thumps the desk three
more times. He fights back tears...*

LUKE: Logout. (*Click.*) Login. (*Click.*) lukestanton92. (*Click.*)
New message. (*Click.*) To dad@heaven.com. Why? Why
won't you speak to me? (*Pause.*) Send. (*Click.*)

*Pause. LUKE closes the computer. Pause, LUKE sitting with his
head in his hands.*

*Quite suddenly, somewhere else in the house, someone begins to
play the piano. Amazed, LUKE listens. After a few seconds, the
music stops in the middle of a bar. Pause. The pianist returns to
the beginning of the piece. We can see the pianist now – a graceful,
silhouetted, ghostly figure playing with great poise and control.
The music stops in the same place. Pause. LUKE walks towards
the piano as the pianist plays the piece again. He recognises the
pianist as his DAD. As the music stops, again in the same place,
the stage is plunged into darkness. LUKE switches on a light. The
pianist is gone. LUKE sits at the piano and plays the same piece.
The pianist appears behind LUKE, watching over his shoulder.
LUKE finds he cannot take the music any further than the ghostly
pianist, and stops in just the same place. Pause. LUKE slams the
piano shut.*

SEQUENCE SIX

*LUKE stands at the bottom of the drainpipe that runs down the side of MRS
LITTLE's house, as in Sequence One. SKIN and DAZ are with him...*

SKIN: Now remember, it's different this time. She's in, so you
got to be quiet.

DAZ: Yeah, quiet as a ickle baby mouse. Squeak!

SKIN: Shut up, Daz.

DAZ: Squeak!

SKIN: Shut up, Daz! (*Pause.*) When you get in, just look for the box, don't muck about with nothing else. All we want right now is the box.

LUKE: What if it's in her bedroom?

SKIN: Then you'll have to be extra quiet, won't you? So as not to wake her up. Go on then, up you go.

Pause. LUKE begins his climb.

That's it. Don't you let us down now, Luke. Cos we're going to be right here waiting for you.

DAZ: Yeah, don't let us down, Luke.

Pause. He climbs through the window and finds himself back on the landing with two closed doors and a flight of stairs leading down. He tentatively approaches the door to NATALIE's room. He puts a hand against the door.

LUKE: Hello?

He twists the doorknob and finds that the room is not locked. He enters the room. The bed is covered with a swirl of bed sheets. LUKE believes NATALIE may be hiding beneath them.

Don't scream. Please don't scream. I won't hurt you, I promise. I'm your friend.

He reaches out and touches the bed sheets. She is not there. Pause. He leaves the room. He approaches the other closed door. The door squeals on its hinges as he opens it. It is another bedroom. A similar swirl of bed sheets on the bed. LUKE sees the box on the other side of the room. He moves silently across to it and picks it up. As he does so, MRS LITTLE appears behind him. She has a stick in one hand and a cordless phone in the other.

MRS LITTLE: Put that down.

LUKE turns to see MRS LITTLE. She is pointing her stick at him.

Don't even think about running, Luke Stanton. You'll only make things worse for yourself. I've phoned the police, they'll be here very soon. (*Pause.*) So, it was you that broke in last night too, was it? She told me you frightened her. (*Pause.*) It's all right, you can come out now, he won't hurt you.

NATALIE appears from the swirl of bed sheets. NATALIE is blind.

I'm here, darling. Nana's here.

NATALIE clings to MRS LITTLE.

It's him. The boy from last night. Don't you want to say hello?

NATALIE clings tighter.

She's been upset all day after your little visit. That's why she's in here with me tonight.

LUKE: I'm not going to hurt her.

MRS LITTLE: I know that. I know you're not like the thugs you're stupid enough to hang around with. (*Pause.*) I didn't really call the police.

LUKE: What?

MRS LITTLE: Say pardon, not what.

LUKE: Sorry.

MRS LITTLE: I said I didn't really call the police. But that's not to say I won't. (*To NATALIE.*) Get into bed now. Good girl.

NATALIE gets into bed. MRS LITTLE tucks her in.

Nana be back very soon. Good girl.

MRS LITTLE walks out of the bedroom.

(To LUKE.) Follow me.

LUKE follows her down the stairs to the kitchen.

Sit down.

LUKE does not sit.

Or run if you like. I'll have phoned the police before you reach the end of the road.

LUKE sits at the kitchen table.

MRS LITTLE: I've been hearing a lot about you and your gang.

LUKE: Who from?

MRS LITTLE: Miss Grubb and her customers. They talk about Jason Skinner and how he's destined for prison. And Darren Fisher and how he bullies money out of the younger children. But mostly they talk about you.

LUKE: What do they say?

MRS LITTLE: They say you're special.

LUKE: Why do they say that?

MRS LITTLE: They say you're gifted. You're Matthew Stanton's son, aren't you? And you play the piano. Like he did.

LUKE: Yeah. Like he did.

MRS LITTLE: I read about the cancer. *(Pause.)* Your father was a wonderful musician. I saw him play ten years ago /

LUKE: I don't want to talk about this /

MRS LITTLE: He was incredible /

LUKE: I just told you, I don't want to talk about this. You deaf or something? I don't want to talk about it. *(Pause.)* I'm going home. Do what you like about the police.

MRS LITTLE: And what about the girl?

LUKE: What about her?

MRS LITTLE: You can help her.

LUKE: How? She's frightened of me.

MRS LITTLE: She's terrified of you.

LUKE: So I can't help, can I?

MRS LITTLE: Stay there.

> *MRS LITTLE hurriedly fetches a tin. She opens the tin and takes out some money. She holds it out to LUKE.*

Take this.

LUKE: What for?

MRS LITTLE: Something to show your friends. I know they're waiting outside for you. When you come back, I'll tell you how you can help.

LUKE: I don't want your money.

MRS LITTLE: Take it.

LUKE: No, and I'm not coming back.

MRS LITTLE: But you have to.

LUKE: Sorry /

MRS LITTLE: She needs you.

LUKE: I can't get involved in this.

MRS LITTLE: She needs your help.

> *LUKE does not take the money. NATALIE comes into the kitchen.*

Please.

NATALIE: Nana…?

MRS LITTLE: Come here, darling.

NATALIE moves across to MRS LITTLE. MRS LITTLE wipes NATALIE's face dry with a handkerchief.

(*To LUKE. Cold.*) Please come back.

*

SKIN and DAZ close in on LUKE.

SKIN: So? What happened?

LUKE: I didn't get the box.

SKIN: We can see that.

LUKE: Well, there was nothing else worth nicking.

DAZ: Yeah, right.

LUKE: Honest. Just a load of ornaments and tacky stuff.

SKIN: Where did you look?

LUKE: Everywhere.

DAZ: What, every room?

LUKE: Yeah.

SKIN: And what about the old woman?

LUKE: Didn't see her.

SKIN: But you went in every room.

LUKE: Yeah /

DAZ: So you must have seen her.

LUKE: Yeah, but what I mean is…

SKIN: What do you mean, Luke?

LUKE: I saw her but she didn't see me, she was asleep.

SKIN: Which room?

LUKE: The one at the top, far side.

DAZ: Was she wearing curlers?

LUKE: No.

DAZ: Bet she looked well ugly /

SKIN: Shut up, Daz. (*Pause. To LUKE.*) Carry on.

LUKE: Nothing more to tell.

SKIN: You sure about that?

    Pause. SKIN grabs LUKE's hands.

LUKE: Come on, Skin /

SKIN: I just want to look at them. (*He studies LUKE's hands.*) Good hands these, Luke. Very good hands. No wonder you're so good at climbing. And playing the piano.

LUKE: Glad you like them. Can I have them back now?

SKIN: Do you click the joints? Daz clicks the joints, makes them pop, don't you, Daz?

DAZ: Sometimes, yeah. (*Pops a knuckle.*)

SKIN: That's it. Can you do that, Luke?

LUKE: No.

SKIN: Doesn't hurt. I'll do it for you.

    SKIN starts pulling on LUKE's fingers.

LUKE: Don't.

SKIN: Keep still. Got to be careful. Else they might break.

LUKE: Please /

SKIN: You're lying to me, Luke.

LUKE: I'm not lying.

SKIN: The old bird was asleep, was she?

LUKE: Yeah.

SKIN: And she didn't wake up?

LUKE: No.

SKIN: So how come the kitchen light went on?

DAZ: Did it?

SKIN: Yes it did, why did the kitchen light come on, Luke?

LUKE: Cos I needed to see better.

SKIN: So why didn't you turn the lights on in the other rooms?

LUKE: Kitchen's the furthest from her bedroom. I didn't want to wake her up. Can you let go of my hands?

SKIN: Why were you in the kitchen so long?

LUKE: Can you let go of my hands?

SKIN: When I'm ready. Why were you in the kitchen so long?

LUKE: I was looking through the drawers. For the box.

Pause. SKIN lets go of LUKE's hands. Pause. He grabs him by the throat.

SKIN: Just remember, you're still in one piece cos that's how I need you right now. And if you want to stay that way, you'll do exactly what I say. Got that?

LUKE: Yeah…

SKIN: Don't you lie to me, Luke, don't you ever lie to me.

LUKE: I'm not.

Pause. SKIN lets go of LUKE.

SKIN: Tomorrow afternoon. Usual time, usual place.

SKIN goes. DAZ follows after SKIN.

SEQUENCE SEVEN

The humming sound returns. LUKE approaches a gravestone and kneels in front of it. The childish tune (Douce Reverie) and the unfinished tune from Sequence Five play in his head, fading in and out, competing for attention. He hears NATALIE's desperate voice: 'Nana, Nana...' The sounds fade away.

*

LUKE turns to see MIRANDA. She is sitting near a piano with her back to him. She is holding her flute.

LUKE: Miranda?

She turns to look at him. She is upset.

I'm sorry.

MIRANDA: What for?

LUKE: Being late.

MIRANDA: Don't apologise. I'm sure you're very busy.

LUKE: It's not that /

MIRANDA: Honestly, it's no big deal. I mean it's a pretty stupid idea anyway, don't you think? You accompanying me. With me being useless and you being brilliant. So, you know, maybe we shouldn't bother /

LUKE: Listen /

MIRANDA: Because I can understand if it's boring for you. But just don't tell me you're going to help me if you don't want to. Because, you know, it might sound silly to you, but this is actually quite important to me /

LUKE: Yeah, but I do want to.

MIRANDA: You don't, you're two hours late /

32

LUKE: But listen, I do. I just… I'm not doing much right at the moment, you know? Something's happening to me, I'm feeling really kind of messed up, I can't explain it.

Pause. MIRANDA's attitude softens.

MIRANDA: Do you want to try?

LUKE: I don't know. My mum's got Roger coming round the whole time, and that's doing my head in. And other stuff too that I can't really talk about.

MIRANDA: It's okay.

LUKE: It's not though, is it? I mean, I didn't mean to make you think like I don't care. (*Pause.*) I was at my dad's grave, that's why I was late. Not cos I don't want to accompany you.

Pause.

MIRANDA: Luke, I'm not going to tell you I understand. Because I don't. But I want to help. So, if you want to talk or anything…

LUKE smiles. Pause.

LUKE: Shall we try the music?

MIRANDA: (*A joke.*) Well, only if you've got time. I mean, since your life's completely falling to pieces /

LUKE: (*He gets the joke.*) I didn't say that /

MIRANDA: Since your life's nothing but a dark pit of despair /

LUKE: Shut up.

MIRANDA: I mean, maybe you should be sorting that out. I don't want you making mistakes and spoiling my beautiful flute-playing, do I?

LUKE sits at the piano.

LUKE: Yeah, right. It'd take more than that to muck up my piano playing. What page is it?

MIRANDA: Twenty-nine.

LUKE finds the music in the book on the piano.

Okay, you're going to have to be really patient with me.

LUKE: That's okay.

MIRANDA: I'll probably stop a lot. And make loads of mistakes and stuff.

LUKE: That's what practice is for.

MIRANDA: I feel kind of nervous with you. I can get through the whole thing, just as long as I don't go too fast.

LUKE: That's all right, it's not meant to be fast. How's this?

LUKE begins to play The Dance of the Blessed Spirits. MIRANDA nods.

(*Over the music.*) Okay, stop and start as much as you like. I'll play around you.

LUKE and MIRANDA play. MIRANDA plays nervously to begin with, but she soon relaxes and plays the piece well.

*

As the music continues, MRS LITTLE signs a letter, puts it in an envelope, seals it and addresses it. The special box is on the table in front of her.

SEQUENCE EIGHT

Again, the laptop computer glows invitingly in the darkness. LUKE moves across and sits at it. He clicks the mouse twice and then types. As before, he speaks the words that he types…

LUKE: Username lukestanton92. Password peanut. (*Click.*) Inbox. Heaven.

LUKE is astonished. For a moment, he is unsure whether he wants to read the email but he decides he must. Click. DANIEL, a man in a suit, appears.

DANIEL: Hello there! We have searched our records and have no record of you contacting us prior to yesterday's email. Would you be so kind as to make your enquiry stroke order again? Thank you and our apologies for any inconvenience, Heaven Scent Natural Perfume Supplies.

LUKE is despondent. Click. DANIEL disappears.

LUKE: Inbox. Kirsti Stanton.

Click. MUM appears.

MUM: I love you, Luke. (*Pause.*) Luke?

LUKE turns in surprise. MUM is really in the room now.

LUKE: Mum.

MUM: Are you hungry? I'll make you a sandwich if you like.

LUKE: No, thanks.

She joins him at the table.

Thanks for the email.

MUM: I meant it.

Pause.

I've never stopped loving your dad. You know that, don't you?

LUKE: Don't.

MUM: What?

LUKE: I can't deal with it. When you talk like this.

MUM: But I want you to understand. I couldn't stop loving him any more than I could stop loving you. But love's a strange thing. You think you've lost it then it creeps up on you again. When your dad died, I really didn't think I'd love again. I don't know, I still don't know how I feel about Roger.

LUKE: You like him.

MUM: Of course I like him.

LUKE: I can tell from how you are with him.

MUM: What do you mean?

LUKE: You're different with him. Excited and stuff. And he's the same. I can hear it in your voices.

MUM: You hear lots of things, don't you? Like your dad. (*Pause.*) I just feel confused more than anything. And guilty that I'm hurting you. But I know your dad would want me to find new love. If that's what made me happy.

LUKE: And does it?

MUM: Not really. Not when I know that it makes you unhappy. Can you imagine a future where it didn't make you unhappy?

LUKE cannot look at her.

Sure you're not hungry?

LUKE does not respond.

It'll be okay. I promise. (*Pause.*) And anyway, I'm not the only one with an admirer.

LUKE looks up.

Don't hurt her feelings, Luke.

LUKE: I won't.

MUM: Miranda's a nice girl.

LUKE: I know.

MUM: She's sensitive. So don't /

LUKE: I won't. She doesn't feel that way about me anyway.

MUM: Oh, right, of course she doesn't. (*She gives him an envelope.*) So who else is hand-posting you letters? Lovely handwriting she's got. Kind of old-fashioned.

MUM goes. LUKE stares at the letter. As he opens it, the computer makes a noise, indicating a new email. He puts the letter down and opens the laptop.

LUKE: Inbox. Jason Skinner. (*Click. SKIN appears.*)

SKIN: Midnight. Be there.

LUKE: (*To the screen.*) I don't think so, Skin. (*Click.*)

SKIN disappears. LUKE closes the laptop, resolute but frightened. He hears the humming sound, very distant, as if its source is somewhere else in the house. He follows the sound. It leads him to his bedroom.

*

As LUKE enters his room, the sound becomes more intense. He hears MIRANDA playing the flute, a harp, rushing water, ravenous insects, MR HARDING mumbling in his sleep. The sounds come together to form an ethereal symphony. He sits on his bed and closes his eyes. The sounds now merge to form the tidal roar and LUKE is flooded by a brilliant blue.

LUKE: The flashes of gold form a circle.
Form a circle round the speck of light.
And we're flying closer now.
And I can see it now.
And it's not just a speck, it's a star.
A five-pointed star.
We're flying towards it.
We're being dragged in.
Bur not just our bodies,
Everything…

The roar becomes euphoric. SKIN and DAZ appear on the street below LUKE's room. SKIN makes a 'fsssst' sound to attract LUKE's attention. He makes the sound several times. The roar implodes and LUKE's head becomes silent.

SKIN: Fsssssst. Luke. Fsssssst.

LUKE opens his window.

LUKE: All right, Skin.

SKIN: (*Hisses.*) What do you think you're playing at? It's one. I said midnight. (*Pause.*) Come on then, are you coming or what? (*Pause.*) I said are you coming or what?!

LUKE: I can't.

SKIN: What did you say?

LUKE: I said I can't come out. I'm not coming.

SKIN is stunned.

SKIN: You're dead, Luke. You are so dead!

SEQUENCE NINE

MRS LITTLE's house. MRS LITTLE regards LUKE with suspicion.

MRS LITTLE: Does anyone know you're here?

LUKE: No.

MRS LITTLE: What about your friends?

LUKE: What friends?

MRS LITTLE: Darren and Jason.

LUKE: They're not my friends.

MRS LITTLE: And what about your mother?

LUKE: She thinks I'm at school.

MRS LITTLE: And what will the school do when you don't turn up?

LUKE: Nothing. They think I'm ill. I emailed the secretary.

MRS LITTLE: And that's acceptable, is it?

LUKE: I sent it from my mum's email account.

MRS LITTLE: No-one can know that you're here.

LUKE: You said in your letter.

MRS LITTLE: (*To herself.*) Good.

LUKE: What?

MRS LITTLE: Don't say what, say pardon. If we're going to spend time together, you'll show me some manners.

LUKE: Who says we're going to spend time together?

MRS LITTLE: Well, you're here now, aren't you?

LUKE: Doesn't mean I'll come again.

MRS LITTLE: That's your choice, but if you don't I'll tell the police about the break-ins. (*Pause.*) I want you to help my granddaughter.

LUKE: How am I supposed to help?

MRS LITTLE: I'll tell you. But first, promise that your visits will remain a secret. You say nothing, I'll say nothing.

LUKE: Fine.

She stares at him.

All right, I promise.

Pause.

MRS LITTLE: Sit down.

LUKE sits.

Natalie has a learning disability. Two years ago, she was in a car crash in which her mother and father were both killed. Since the crash she's become very confused and frightened. She's unsure of everything, who she is, who her parents were, who I am /

LUKE: She calls you Nana.

MRS LITTLE: I taught her that but she doesn't understand what it means.

Pause.

LUKE: Has she always been blind?

MRS LITTLE: No, that happened in the crash. She was blinded by glass from the windscreen.

Pause. LUKE stands as if to leave.

LUKE: This isn't my problem /

MRS LITTLE: I'm not finished yet, let me finish!

Reluctantly, LUKE sits.

Ever since the crash, she's been living here.

LUKE: She's been living here two whole years?

MRS LITTLE: Yes, but she's not been out of the house in that time.

LUKE: In two years? Why not?

MRS LITTLE: It would frighten her. And besides, I'm not supposed to have her.

Pause.

LUKE: What do you mean?

Pause.

MRS LITTLE: When the accident happened I was living in India. I'd been a nurse there. I couldn't get a flight to England until after the funeral, by which time Natalie was in a home. She was receiving a level of care that I didn't consider adequate, so I took her away.

LUKE: What, you stole her?

MRS LITTLE: It was in her best interests.

LUKE: But you're related. They would have let you take her anyway.

MRS LITTLE: They would have said an old woman like me couldn't cope with Natalie's special needs. Well, that's a joke if you've seen the home she was in. She needs constant attention.

LUKE: Is that why you don't go out? I thought you just didn't like people very much.

MRS LITTLE: I don't.

Pause.

LUKE: I still don't see how I can help.

MRS LITTLE: I want you to play for her. You're very good, I'm told.

LUKE: How's me playing the piano going to help?

Pause.

MRS LITTLE: I hired a piano-tuner. Once he'd finished tuning, he played. She could hear it from her room. It made her happy. I'd never seen her so peaceful.

LUKE: Can't you just put the radio on?

MRS LITTLE: It doesn't have the same effect.

LUKE: Why have you got a piano if you can't play?

MRS LITTLE: That's none of your business.

LUKE: And why keep it tuned if no-one uses it?

MRS LITTLE: You're not here to ask questions, you're here to play.

LUKE: Is that an order?

Pause.

MRS LITTLE: No. It's a request. I would like it if you would play. For my granddaughter.

LUKE sits at the piano.

LUKE: What do you want me to play?

MRS LITTLE: Anything. Anything you like.

LUKE plays the piano. MRS LITTLE leaves the room. He plays alone. After a few moments, NATALIE comes into the room, fragile and dishevelled. LUKE senses her presence. He stops playing and turns. They look at one another. Interval.

SEQUENCE TEN

MRS LITTLE's house, a few minutes later. LUKE is playing Pavane by Ravel. MRS LITTLE and NATALIE stand together. They listen absorbedly. The music comes to an end. Pause.

MRS LITTLE: I'll make some tea. You'll stay and play some more, won't you? You'd like to hear some more, wouldn't you, Natalie?

NATALIE wants more music. MRS LITTLE goes to make tea.

LUKE: Hello, Natalie.

NATALIE backs away from the piano.

It's all right. I'll play some more, shall I? I'll play some more.

LUKE plays Nocturne by Grieg. As the music progresses, NATALIE edges towards LUKE. He senses her moving in and plays especially softly so as not to distress her. NATALIE plays a note on the piano. She plays the note a few times, getting louder. LUKE stops playing.

Do you want to play?

NATALIE reaches out and touches LUKE's face.

NATALIE: Ears…

42

LUKE: That's right. They're my ears.

NATALIE: Funny…

LUKE: You find them funny?

NATALIE: Funny ears.

LUKE: Maybe I find your ears funny.

He touches her ear but she recoils.

Don't worry. I won't hurt you.

He puts a hand on her shoulder. She moves closer and snuggles against him. They stay like this for a little while. He looks up and sees a clock on the wall.

Four o'clock… Miranda! (*He gets up to leave.*) Natalie, I'll come back soon, okay? I'll come back and play again soon. (*Calls out.*) Mrs Little, I've got to go.

MRS LITTLE: (*Off.*) I beg your pardon.

LUKE: I'm late, I've got to go.

MRS LITTLE: (*Off.*) But I've made tea.

LUKE: Yeah, sorry. I'll come back soon, I promise.

LUKE leaves NATALIE at the piano. She runs her hands across the keys.

*

Outside LUKE's house. LUKE is hurriedly walking past on his way to meet MIRANDA. A light is switched on in an upstairs room. He looks up to see his DAD, standing at the window, looking down at him.

LUKE: Dad?

DAD disappears to be replaced by ROGER. ROGER does not see LUKE. He is joined by MUM. He kisses her tenderly. MUM draws a curtain, shutting LUKE out.

*

The graveyard. LUKE sits by his DAD's headstone, deep in tortured thought. MIRANDA appears.

MIRANDA: I thought I'd find you here. Are you all right? (*LUKE doesn't reply.*) Luke? You weren't in school. Are you ill or something?

LUKE: No.

MIRANDA: Only…you said you'd come over for a rehearsal. I thought maybe /

LUKE: What, that I'd stood you up again?

MIRANDA: No, just that something might be wrong. So I came to look for you. I went to your tree. I would have phoned but I didn't want to get you in trouble. If, like, your mum didn't know you weren't in school or something.

LUKE buries his face in his hands and cries. For a moment, MIRANDA is not sure what to do. She sits next to LUKE and puts an arm around him. He stops crying.

What is it? Is it Jason Skinner? He was asking where you were today. Has he…done something to you?

LUKE: Not yet.

MIRANDA: What does that mean?

LUKE: It doesn't matter. It's not them anyway.

MIRANDA: Then what is it?

LUKE: It's not the same any more.

MIRANDA: What isn't?

LUKE: With mum.

MIRANDA: In what way?

LUKE: I saw them just now. Kissing. I was walking past the house on the way to yours. They were in the window.

MIRANDA: Did they see you?

LUKE: No. It's just... I can't deal with that. It's not right. And the way it looked. I can't deal with it.

Pause.

MIRANDA: Luke, I know you don't want to hear this right now, but Roger's a nice man.

LUKE: My dad was a nice man.

MIRANDA: I know. (*Pause.*) Okay, if your dad was here now, if you could ask him about your mum and Roger, what do you think he'd say?

LUKE: Well, he's not here, is he?

MIRANDA: Yeah, but just imagine /

LUKE: But he's not! He's gone! That's what happens when you die, you disappear! (*Pause.*) I'm sorry.

MIRANDA: It's okay.

LUKE: I shouldn't have shouted.

MIRANDA: I'm fine.

LUKE: What's the matter with me?! (*Pause.*) Do you want to go and rehearse?

MIRANDA: Only if you want to. I mean, if you'd rather just go home...

LUKE: Go home? What would I want to go there for? (*He stands and helps her up.*) Come on. We'll get an hour in before tea if we go now.

SEQUENCE ELEVEN

LUKE's bedroom. He is exhausted. He enjoys a rare moment of peace. He hears the opening phrase of Reverie. He hums it back to himself.

LUKE: I know that tune…

He hums the tune again, getting a few notes further into the tune. A light comes up on the piano. DAD is at the piano. He plays the first note.

I'm at the old house.

DAD plays the note again.

I must be four years old…

LUKE hums Reverie and DAD plays with him. The light on the piano gets warmer, sunnier as DAD continues to play and LUKE speaks…

It's summer.
All the windows open.
Dad doesn't know I'm there.
I'm standing in the hallway.
I don't want it to stop.
Ever.
And that's the tune he's playing.
And when it finishes, I run into the room.
And he picks me up,
Says, 'Did you like that, Luke?'
And I say, 'Yes.'
And he says, 'Then it's for you.'

SKIN and DAZ appear in the street.

SKIN: Oi!

Abruptly, the music stops, the piano slams shut and DAD is plunged into darkness. Pause.

Oi!

DAZ: Quiet, Skin, his mum'll hear.

SKIN: I don't care who hears!

LUKE does not go to the window.

I know you're in there, Luke! Well, you listen to me. You can't hide away forever. Your time's going to come. And when I catch you, I swear, you'll wish you never crossed me. Worst mistake of your life, Luke Stanton. Worst mistake of your life!

*

NATALIE is crying.

SEQUENCE TWELVE

The kitchen. MUM is sitting at the table, working on her laptop. The phone rings. She answers it.

MUM: Hello?

Pause.

Hello?

She replaces the receiver. This is not the first time this has happened. She is anxious. LUKE comes in.

LUKE: Morning.

MUM: Do you know anything about that?

LUKE: About what?

MUM: Happened twice yesterday too. The phone rings, I pick it up and say hello, the line goes dead.

LUKE: Probably some bored nutcase.

MUM: Either that or Jason Skinner. What's going on?

LUKE: Nothing.

MUM: Don't lie to me.

LUKE: I'm not. It's not Skin, it's nothing to do with me.

MUM: You're out all the time, you never tell me where you're going, I sometimes even wonder if you're coming back.

LUKE: Well, what time did you get back last night? It was after I went to bed.

Pause. She is upset.

Mum…

MUM: It's over, okay?

LUKE: What is?

MUM: With Roger.

LUKE: When?

MUM: Last night. That's why I was late back.

Pause.

LUKE: How? What happened?

MUM: Nothing happened.

LUKE: Did he do something to hurt you?

MUM: Of course he didn't.

LUKE: Then…why?

MUM: I just decided. For everyone. So you can stop hating him now.

She turns from him and busies herself. LUKE hears the humming sound. He presses a finger against the side of his head. She turns back and watches him for a moment.

Your dad used to do that. Touch his head when he was hearing something unusual. You're so like him. You even hear the same sounds.

LUKE: How do you know about the sounds I can hear?

MUM: Your dad told me.

LUKE: I never told him.

The sound begins to build.

MUM: You didn't need to. He could tell. I'd wake up in the
night and he'd be lying there, eyes closed, dead still but
awake. And I'd ask him what he was hearing and he'd say
bells or strings or buzzing or rushing water. Or sometimes
he'd hear complete pieces of music, some of them pieces
he'd never heard before. But most often, it was a kind of
humming or roaring sound. He said that sound was all the
other sounds added together. He called it the engine. He
said it was the engine that started creation and keeps things
running. But he didn't like telling people about the sounds.
He only ever really told me and Mr Harding. He said the
sounds were sacred, and if he talked too much, he thought
they might leave him.

LUKE: I don't like talking about it either. But not because of
that, just because I don't want people thinking I'm off my
head.

MUM smiles. The sound dies away. Pause.

MUM: I'll tell you one thing he said. One night, I found him
at the kitchen table with some paper and some crayons.
He was cradling you in his left arm and he was drawing a
picture. And he was crying.

LUKE: Dad was crying?

MUM: Tears pouring down his face. He said he was as happy
as he'd ever been. And then he said, 'The firmament is
singing.'

LUKE: What does that mean?

MUM: The firmament? It means the sky and everything in it.
The sun, the moon, the stars. And it kind of means heaven
as well.

LUKE: What was the picture of?

MUM: It was a picture of the sounds in his head. He said he could draw sounds because sounds have colours and shapes /

LUKE: But the picture. It was a five-pointed star, wasn't it?

MUM: (*Amazed but not shocked.*) Yeah. (*Pause.*) He'd say everything in creation had a song of its own and, if you listened hard, you could hear them.

LUKE: Can we stop now?

MUM smiles sympathetically.

MUM: Okay.

MUM moves to leave the kitchen.

LUKE: Mum, this thing with Roger...

MUM: It's over.

LUKE: Completely?

MUM: Completely. It's just you and me now.

MUM goes. LUKE opens the laptop. He is surprised to find MUM's email account open.

LUKE: Inbox. Roger Gillmore.

He gives in to temptation. Click. ROGER appears.

ROGER: Don't be sorry, Kirsti. I know you're hurting too. I understand that Luke comes first.

Pause. Click. ROGER disappears.

LUKE: New message. (*Click.*) To admin@priory9.sch.uk. Dear Mrs Jay, I'm sorry but Luke is still ill so I've decided to keep him home another day. Kirsti Stanton. Send. (*Click.*)

*

Recorded music: Peace of the Forest

SEQUENCE THIRTEEN

LUKE is playing Peace of the Forest for NATALIE, who is sitting on the floor. MRS LITTLE stands nearby. After a short while, NATALIE speaks…

NATALIE: Trees.

LUKE: (*Continuing to play.*) Trees? Is that what you can see?

NATALIE: And leaves.

LUKE: You're like me. I see music too.

NATALIE: Sunshine.

> *LUKE finishes the piece. He looks through a book of sheet music for something new to play…*

LUKE: So she can remember things she's seen, from before the accident?

MRS LITTLE: Some things, yes. But I don't know how much.

LUKE: Does she know my name?

MRS LITTLE: I've told her it but I don't suppose she took it in.

LUKE: Do you know my name, Natalie?

NATALIE: Funny ears.

LUKE: Oh, is that my name? I thought my name was Luke.

MRS LITTLE: She'd be more likely to remember if you didn't leave it so long between visits.

LUKE: I was here yesterday morning.

MRS LITTLE: It was yesterday afternoon she needed you. She was all right for a couple of hours after you went, but then the crying started. It took all day to calm her down. (*Pause.*) If I make some tea, will you stay to drink it this time?

LUKE: Thanks.

> *MRS LITTLE goes. LUKE turns away from the piano.*

What else can you remember from before the accident? (*Pause.*) Can you remember where you lived? The name of the village?

He sits with her on the floor.

Can you remember your second name? Or if you had any brothers or sisters? (*Pause.*) No? (*Pause.*) Shall I play some more?

LUKE moves to play the piano but NATALIE clings tight to him and squeals.

Hey, it's all right, it's okay, I'm not going anywhere. We can keep talking if you like.

NATALIE hums the first six notes of Reverie but it is slurred and unrecognisable.

What's that? Are you singing to me?

She sings again. This time, LUKE recognises the tune. Pause.

Sing that again for me.

She sings again. It is clearer still.

I know that tune. I think about that tune a lot. Normally when I think about you.

LUKE sings the notes back to her. NATALIE repeats them.

That tune, what's it called?

NATALIE: Bar-ley.

LUKE: Barley?

NATALIE: Barley.

LUKE: Is that what you see when you hear it? I can see a star. An amazing five-pointed star.

He sings the notes again. She starts to cry.

NATALIE: Barley, barley!

LUKE: It's all right.

NATALIE: Barley!

LUKE: It's all right, I can see it too now. A field of barley swaying in the breeze. That's what I can see. It's all right, don't be sad.

NATALIE: Barley!

She goes. He calls after her.

LUKE: Don't go, it's all right…

Sequence ends.

*

LUKE's head is invaded by a growing noise: a disjointed music of horns, bells and flutes; a piercing whistle like an old fashioned kettle; wood being chopped; the hum and the roar. The noise continues into…

SEQUENCE FOURTEEN

MR HARDING's room.

HARDING: What's the matter?

LUKE: I can hear sounds. Everywhere.

HARDING: I know you can.

LUKE: Can you hear them?

HARDING: No.

LUKE: It's not horrible.

HARDING: I know.

LUKE: It's just weird.

The sound reaches a climax and disappears.

Mum told me Dad heard the same things. Like the jumble of instruments. And the roar. She said he talked to you about it.

HARDING: He did. He said it was the primal force that drives the cosmos and everything that exists.

LUKE: How though?

HARDING: Through vibration. All matter is in a constant state of vibration. Or, as your dad would put it, every stick, stone, cloud, animal or person has its own unique song, and that's what you're hearing. And he'd say thoughts have vibrations too, and feelings and desires. He'd say he could hear love or anger. And other sounds too, of forces and ideas beyond human imagination.

LUKE: I don't really understand.

HARDING: I think you understand better than you realise. You certainly understand better than I ever could. You hear the sounds, I never will.

LUKE: But you believe in them.

HARDING: Only because I heard your dad speak about them. (*Pause.*) Your dad, Luke, was an extraordinary man. He was just the same as you. Just as sensitive, just as easily hurt, just as musical /

LUKE: More musical.

HARDING: No, about the same, I'd say. And he'd agree. (*Pause.*) Do you see things too? Do sounds have colours and shapes?

LUKE: Sometimes.

HARDING: (*Plays a B flat on the piano.*) B flat. What colour do you see?

LUKE: Green?

HARDING: (*Plays a B major chord.*) And what's that?

LUKE: It's a B major chord.

HARDING: What colour?

LUKE: Bright red. B flat major I get a mixture. Like bits of blue and bits of yellow. Did my dad see colours too?

HARDING: I think he did. Maybe not the same colours, but who knows?

Pause.

LUKE: Mr Harding, there was one other thing.

HARDING: Yes?

LUKE: A tune. I can't figure out what it is.

HARDING: Play the melody for me.

LUKE: It's been haunting me.

LUKE plays the first few notes of Reverie.

HARDING: Again.

He plays them again.

HARDING: That's Douce Reverie by Tchaikovsky.

LUKE: Have you got it?

HARDING: I think so.

MR HARDING searches for the music.

And what colour is Douce Reverie, Luke?

LUKE: It's deep blue. Like the sea.

HARDING: And what else?

LUKE: Gold? With a speck of light in the centre.

HARDING: Just a speck of light? Not a star? (*Pause.*) Your dad saw it too.

LUKE: What is it?

HARDING: I asked him the same question. He said it was a symbol of the primal sound. And the gateway to another world.

He gives LUKE the music.

SEQUENCE FIFTEEN

NATALIE is crying.

*

The crying continues as the phone begins to ring in LUKE's kitchen. LUKE comes into the kitchen, still holding the sheet music from MR HARDING, and picks up the phone. MRS LITTLE appears.

LUKE: Hello?

MRS LITTLE: Luke. You need to come over.

LUKE: What?

MRS LITTLE: You heard me.

LUKE: I've only just got in.

MRS LITTLE: I don't care. She needs you.

LUKE: But /

MRS LITTLE: It's never been this bad. Can you hear her?

LUKE: I've been hearing her all day.

MRS LITTLE: What do you mean?

LUKE: Nothing.

MRS LITTLE: Just hurry up. She needs you.

MRS LITTLE disappears. LUKE hangs up and goes, taking the sheet music with him. The crying stops abruptly.

*

LUKE is walking over the bridge that passes over the brook. He drops the sheet music. As he gathers it up, SKIN appears on the grass beneath. DAZ follows shortly after. LUKE listens to their conversation.

DAZ: See. I told you he wouldn't be here.

SKIN: No you didn't.

DAZ: I said, 'He won't be by the brook, it's too obvious.'

SKIN: Shut up, Daz.

DAZ: He's out-thinking you, Skin.

SKIN: What?!

DAZ: Nothing. Sorry, Skin.

Pause.

SKIN: He's like a little worm, he keeps slipping through my fingers /

DAZ laughs loudly.

What are you laughing at?

DAZ: Worm!

DAZ sees that SKIN is unimpressed and falls silent.

So what are you going to do, Skin?

SKIN: When?

DAZ: When we find him. Going to give him a good kicking?

SKIN: No. I've got way more interesting plans than that.

DAZ: Yeah?

SKIN: Yeah. I'm planning something big. Come on.

DAZ and SKIN move on. LUKE finishes gathering his sheet music and continues on his way to MRS LITTLE's house.

*

NATALIE is at the piano, thumping the keys and crying. MRS LITTLE, herself in a state of some distress, leads LUKE into the room.

MRS LITTLE: She won't eat, she won't sleep, she just keeps crying. Natalie, it's Luke, he'll play for you.

LUKE: I'll play for you, shall I, Natalie? I've got some music I think you might like.

LUKE hurriedly props the sheet music on the piano and begins to play Reverie. The effect on NATALIE is almost instant. She stops crying.

There. That's better, isn't it? You like this one, don't you?

The effect of the music on NATALIE is almost hypnotic. She sits on the floor to listen. Before long, she is curled in a ball on the floor, asleep. MRS LITTLE sits. The music comes to an end. LUKE turns and looks at NATALIE.

MRS LITTLE: Thank you.

LUKE: That's all right.

MRS LITTLE: It's the worst she's been. If you hadn't come I don't know what I would have done.

LUKE: Do you want me to carry her upstairs?

MRS LITTLE: Would you?

LUKE picks NATALIE up.

LUKE: Come on, you need some sleep.

MRS LITTLE: Put her in my bed for now.

LUKE: You look pretty tired as well.

MRS LITTLE: I'll rest down here.

LUKE takes NATALIE up the stairs to MRS LITTLE's bedroom. He carefully puts her into bed and tucks her in.

LUKE: Get some sleep, eh?

He is about to leave the room when he sees MRS LITTLE's black velvet box. Silently, furtively, he walks across to the box and opens it. He takes out a framed photograph and studies it. He puts the photograph down and takes out a letter. Squadron Leader JAMES P HUTCHINSON appears.

HUTCHINSON: Dear Mrs Little, it is with great regret that I write to inform you that Bill was shot down earlier today by enemy aircraft. I am sorry to say there is no possibility that he could have survived. It grieves me immensely to be the bearer of such dreadful news. Bill was a wonderful man, greatly respected by all of us here, and he will be sorely missed. I enclose a framed photograph of you both that was found among his things. The rest of his effects will, of course, be sent to you. Once again, I am so sorry to have to give you such shattering news. Yours sincerely, Squadron Leader James P Hutchinson.

LUKE puts the letter on the table. He sees something else in the box – an identity bracelet.

LUKE: (*Reads from the bracelet.*) 'Barley May Roberts.'

MRS LITTLE stands and heads upstairs.

'Barley May Roberts.'

MRS LITTLE is not far from the bedroom…

MRS LITTLE: Luke.

LUKE hurriedly puts the letter and the picture back in the box. He pockets the bracelet a second before MRS LITTLE comes into the room.

Is everything all right?

Pause.

LUKE: Yeah.

Pause.

MRS LITTLE: Good. You can go then, if you want to.

SEQUENCE SIXTEEN

Night. LUKE sits at the kitchen table. The laptop is closed in front of him. He stares at the bracelet. He closes his eyes and takes some deep breaths.

LUKE: I know you're there, Dad. I can feel you there. I'm just trying to do the best thing. You know that, don't you?

He opens his eyes and opens the laptop.

Search. (*Click. Types…*) Barley May Roberts. (*Click.*) 'Barley May Roberts Official Website.' (*Click.*)

MRS ROBERTS appears.

MRS ROBERTS: We haven't seen our beautiful daughter, Barley May Roberts, for two years now. She went missing on a trip to St Peter's Park, outside Hastings, on June 17th 2005. Our attention was distracted away from her for just a few seconds, and in that time she disappeared. Now ten years old, Barley is a friendly and trusting girl. She was born with a learning disability and she attended Rose Hill Special School. Here is a photo of Barley taken shortly before her disappearance.

LUKE: Natalie…

MRS ROBERTS: Please, if you have any information, call the number below.

LUKE picks up the phone and dials the number. We hear the phone ring several times, and then a connection…

Hello? (*Pause.*) Hello? (*Pause.*) Fine, if you're not going to speak /

LUKE: Wait!

Pause.

MRS ROBERTS: Who is this? (*Pause.*) If you've got something to say, then say it. If you're a hoax caller, you're certainly not the first. (*Pause.*) Okay /

LUKE: No, wait, are you Mrs Roberts?

MRS ROBERTS: Who is this?

LUKE: It's about Barley. I know where she is, and this isn't a hoax, so just listen, all right?

MRS ROBERTS: Where is she?

LUKE: She's safe. I promise, I've seen her /

MRS ROBERTS: But where is she?

LUKE: Mrs Roberts, does Barley have any grandparents?

MRS ROBERTS: No, why? (*Pause.*) Listen, whoever you are, she's our daughter /

LUKE: I know that, and I'm going to help, you just have to listen, all right? Hear me out.

MR ROBERTS appears.

MR ROBERTS: Who is it?

MRS ROBERTS: It's about Barley.

LUKE: Mrs Roberts, you've got to do what I say, all right? Okay, did you know...because it doesn't say anything on the website... When you last saw Barley was she blind?

MRS ROBERTS: She's blind?!

MR ROBERTS: What have you done to her?!

LUKE: Nothing!

MR ROBERTS: Who the hell are you?!

MRS ROBERTS: Stop it /

MR ROBERTS: What have you done?!

MRS ROBERTS: Please /

LUKE: I haven't done anything!

MR ROBERTS: If you've hurt her, I will find you, I will find you!

LUKE: Stop it, I'm trying to help!

Pause.

MRS ROBERTS: Are you still there?

LUKE: Yes.

MRS ROBERTS: You have to understand... We're in a terrible state over this, and we've had so many false alarms, and now you're telling us that she's blind...

LUKE: I know, I'm sorry. (*Pause.*) But I promise you, this isn't a false alarm, I'll describe her to you. She's got /

MRS ROBERTS: There's a photo on the website. How do we know that you're not just describing the photo.

LUKE: All right, I'll hum you a tune. Do you recognise this tune?

LUKE hums Reverie. MRS ROBERTS breaks down.

MR ROBERTS: What's he doing?

MRS ROBERTS: He's humming the tune.

MR ROBERTS: What tune?

MRS ROBERTS: Reverie.

LUKE stops humming.

MR ROBERTS: Just tell us what we have to do.

SEQUENCE SEVENTEEN

MRS LITTLE's house. BARLEY is on the floor, sobbing. LUKE has just arrived at the house.

MRS LITTLE: I didn't expect you until late this afternoon. Aren't you supposed to be at school?

LUKE: I didn't go.

MRS LITTLE: Won't you get in trouble?

LUKE: Probably. How did she sleep?

MRS LITTLE: She slept right through after you left. But then she woke up around five and started with all this moaning and weeping. She hasn't stopped since.

LUKE crouches by BARLEY and strokes her hair.

LUKE: Hi, Natalie. Remember me?

She clings to LUKE. She holds his ears.

That's right. Funny ears.

He hums Reverie to BARLEY. She stops crying.

Good girl. No more tears.

MRS LITTLE: You obviously have the magic touch.

LUKE: Yeah.

Pause, LUKE stroking BARLEY's hair.

Mrs Little…

MRS LITTLE: Yes?

LUKE: Could I have a drink, please?

MRS LITTLE: I'll get you some orange juice.

LUKE: Yeah, could I have something hot? Anything will do. Cup of tea, hot chocolate, whatever.

Pause.

MRS LITTLE: I'll make some hot chocolate. Natalie likes hot chocolate.

LUKE: With lots of sugar, please.

Pause.

MRS LITTLE: How many spoonfuls?

LUKE: What?

MRS LITTLE: I told you, I don't like it when you say what.

LUKE: Sorry.

MRS LITTLE: How many spoonfuls of sugar?

LUKE: Two, please.

MRS LITTLE goes. Silently, LUKE picks BARLEY up.

(*Whispers.*) Quiet now, Barley. I'm taking you home.

LUKE checks that it is safe to go and leaves with BARLEY.

*

LUKE is carrying BARLEY through the forest.

LUKE: You okay, Barley?

BARLEY: Trees.

LUKE: Can you hear the trees?

BARLEY: Hear the trees…

LUKE: We're going to stop here, okay?

LUKE stops and puts BARLEY down.

BARLEY: Barley.

LUKE: That's right. That's your name, isn't it? Barley May Roberts. I'm just going to make a phone call, okay?

LUKE takes out a mobile phone and dials. MR and MRS ROBERTS appear.

MRS ROBERTS: Yes?

LUKE: It's me. Are you in Bramblebury yet?

MRS ROBERTS: Yes. We're by a thatched cottage with a white gate.

LUKE: Good. Head north along that road.

MRS ROBERTS: Towards Upper Dinton?

LUKE: That's it. You'll be driving along the edge of Buckland Forest. After a while there'll be a layby on your left. It's by a field with loads of buttercups in it. Pull in there and wait.

MRS ROBERTS: And then you'll phone?

LUKE: Yes.

MRS ROBERTS: But you will phone, won't you?

LUKE: Yes, I'll phone. I promise you, Mrs Roberts, you'll have Barley back very soon.

MR and MRS ROBERTS disappear. LUKE goes back to BARLEY. He strokes her hair.

Only me. Are you all right?

BARLEY: Singing.

LUKE: Who's singing?

BARLEY: Trees.

LUKE: The trees are singing. I think you're right. There's lots of different trees around here, all singing different songs. There's a tree over there that's mine.

He points BARLEY's arm in the direction of his tree.

Me and my dad put a tree-house in it. (*Pause.*) Now listen, Barley. I want you to know that I'll always be thinking about you, and I'll always love you. And so will Nana. And mummy and daddy will always love you too. They're going to be here very soon, okay? And they're going to look after you again.

LUKE begins to hum Reverie. BARLEY joins in.

That's it. Keep humming. I'm just going over here for a while. Keep humming.

BARLEY keeps humming. LUKE dials. MR and MRS ROBERTS appear.

Mrs Roberts.

MRS ROBERTS: Yes?

LUKE: Okay. Get out of the car.

MRS ROBERTS: Yes.

LUKE: And cross the road.

MR ROBERTS: What's he saying?

MRS ROBERTS: Cross the road.

LUKE: Can you see a path into the forest?

MRS ROBERTS: Yes.

LUKE: Go down there. (*Pause.*) Are you on the path?

MRS ROBERTS: Yes.

LUKE: Keep walking. (*Pause.*) Keep walking. (*Pause.*) Okay, I'm going to go now /

MRS ROBERTS: No, don't go /

LUKE: I have to go, but keep walking and very soon you'll see her. But please don't rush and don't call out, okay? Goodbye.

LUKE hangs up. Pause.

MR ROBERTS: Barley?

MR and MRS ROBERTS slowly approach BARLEY, being careful not to frighten her. They are drained but elated. They kneel with her and hold her. LUKE looks on from behind a tree. They take her away. A happy, warm, exhilarating noise begins to emanate from the trees.

LUKE: The trees are singing.

The noise builds. It is coming from everywhere now, especially the sky. LUKE looks up in wonder.

The firmament is singing.

*

*The sound continues as SKIN and DAZ arrive, unseen by LUKE.
DAZ grabs LUKE from behind and turns him round to face SKIN,
holding his arms, restricting his movement.*

SKIN: Thought we were in school, did you?

LUKE: Skin /

SKIN: Well, you got that wrong didn't you?

SKIN grabs LUKE's face.

Stupid thing is, Luke, none of this needed to happen, did
it? You only had to do what we agreed. But you went and
let us down, didn't you? And then you stopped showing
respect. And that's not something we ever forgive.

*SKIN takes a cigarette lighter out and snaps it open. A big flame.
He waves it close to LUKE's face.*

DAZ: Skin…

SKIN: What?

DAZ: I reckon he's learnt his lesson.

SKIN: Well, I don't.

DAZ: Come on…

SKIN: Just shut up and hold him or I'll do you and all!

*DAZ holds LUKE. SKIN slowly runs the flame down LUKE's
arm*

I told you, Luke. I told you what would happen if you
messed with me. I warned you and you can't say I didn't.

*SKIN takes hold of one of LUKE's hands. He teases it with the
flame.*

That's the thing with piano players, I suppose. Need a
good pair of hands. Your hands insured, Lukey?

LUKE says nothing.

Oh, that's a shame, cos after today you won't be playing piano again. In fact, you ain't going to be doing anything. That's right /

DAZ: Skin, listen /

SKIN: Shut up, Daz.

DAZ: But do we have to?

SKIN: Shut up, I said! We agreed!

SKIN starts to burn LUKE's hand. LUKE struggles.

Such pretty hands. I bet your dad had pretty hands.

LUKE pulls free of DAZ. SKIN tries to grab him but LUKE wrestles free, pushing SKIN to the ground. LUKE runs off.

Well, don't just stand there!

DAZ: Eh?

SKIN: Go on!

They chase him.

*

LUKE is climbing the tree. SKIN arrives just too late as LUKE pulls himself beyond his reach, apparently to safety. He reaches his tree-house.

SKIN: Don't think you're going to be safe up there. Because you're not. This is the day you're going to die.

DAZ arrives.

Come on, Daz, get to work.

DAZ starts to bring tyres and branches from a hiding place nearby. He heaps them around the foot of the tree.

We thought you might try something like this so we made a few preparations. So, you might as well sit back and relax, Luke. Enjoy your last few moments on earth.

LUKE takes out his mobile and dials.

LUKE: Mum, I'm in trouble /

SKIN: Ahh, he's phoning his mum /

LUKE: If you get this message /

SKIN: Bless!

LUKE: I'm in the forest, in my tree, Skin's going to kill me, don't come on your own.

LUKE dials a different number.

SKIN: That's the stuff, Daz. Pile it nice and high. This is going to be fun, don't you reckon, Luke?

LUKE: Roger, it's Luke, I'm in trouble, I'm in the tree-house, please come and help.

SKIN: All right, Daz, that'll do. Now, get the diesel.

DAZ: Skin /

SKIN: Get it!

DAZ fetches a can of diesel. SKIN takes if off him. He pours it on the tyres and branches around the tree.

What we have here, Luke, is diesel. Specially for you. And with these tyres it's going to make quite a lot of thick, black smoke. Not very nice to breathe in. Going to finish you off, it is. And your precious tree. I warned you, Luke.

DAZ runs off.

I warned you!

SKIN holds the lighter to the diesel…

LUKE: No…

SKIN sets light to the tree and runs off after DAZ.

No…!

The fire builds quickly, cracking and roaring. Thick smoke billows from it.

Help! Somebody please! Help me! Help! Anyone! Please!

LUKE begins to cough.

Help! Help!

He wipes the tears from his eyes and the spit from his mouth.

Smoke.
Black smoke and so much of it.
My eyes are burning,
My lungs are like fists,
My mouth is…aching for air!

The roar of the fire becomes deafening, drowning LUKE out. It reaches a powerful, almost deafening crescendo and LUKE suddenly finds himself at the centre of an entirely different, altogether woozier world of unfamiliar, muffled, heavenly noise.

I'm falling.
But at the same time going up.
Flying up through my tree,
Past the branches,
Through the leaves,
Out into the sky.
I can breathe up here.
I can breathe.
And I can see my own body
Sprawled out on the ground.

A blissful light shines on LUKE, growing brighter and brighter.

There's a star up above me and it speaks:
'Are you ready to die?
Or are you ready to live?'

The world becomes silent.

I think of Mum.
And Miranda.
And Mrs Little
And Barley
And Mr Harding.
And I think of Dad.
I'm ready to live.

The deafening noise returns…

I'm ready to live!

LUKE is plunged into darkness but the noise continues, roaring, rattling and crackling to a climax.

SEQUENCE EIGHTEEN

A hospital room. LUKE is asleep in a hospital bed. ROGER is by the bed, his arm in a sling. LUKE wakes up. Moving and speaking is painful for him.

LUKE: Roger. Where am I?

ROGER: In hospital.

LUKE: (*Tries to sit up.*) Eh?

ROGER: Take it easy, you're not in a good way.

LUKE: What happened?

ROGER: Don't you remember?

LUKE thinks.

LUKE: I remember being stuck up the tree. And all the smoke. And I kind of remember…lying on the ground, talking to you.

ROGER: That's right, we were waiting for the ambulance.

LUKE: Yeah. You looked after me. How did you get hurt?

ROGER: Me? Don't worry about me. Just a couple of scratches. It's you we've all been worried about.

LUKE: Yeah… Thanks, Roger.

MUM comes into the room.

MUM: You're awake.

LUKE: Hello, Mum.

MUM: How are you feeling?

LUKE: I've felt better.

MUM: I'm not surprised.

ROGER: I'll leave you two alone, shall I?

LUKE: Stay.

ROGER: No, I'll go, I'll be back in a bit.

ROGER goes. Pause.

MUM: Silly boy.

LUKE: I phoned you, didn't I? When I was in the tree-house.

MUM: I was on the phone to Mrs Jay. She was asking me when you'd be well enough to come back to school.

LUKE: Sorry.

MUM: It doesn't matter now.

LUKE: What happened? I can remember…like a figure running forward as I fell…

MUM: That was Roger. He got your message and ran down just in time to see you falling. He got underneath you to cushion your fall.

LUKE: Must have hurt.

MUM: I think it did, he broke his wrist and put his shoulder out. And then he had to drag you away from the smoke, by which time you'd stopped breathing, so he gave you CPR. He saved your life.

LUKE: I always said he was a nice bloke.

MUM smiles.

Who called the ambulance?

MUM: Darren Fisher. It seems like he had an attack of conscience.

Pause.

LUKE: I'm so sorry, Mum.

MUM: It's all right.

LUKE: I'll make things better, I promise.

MUM: It's okay. There's nothing broken that can't be fixed.

LUKE: I will, I'll make it all better. (*Pause.*) You'd better marry him after all this. What else has a bloke got to do?

MUM smiles.

SEQUENCE NINETEEN

LUKE sits at the piano. He splays his fingers in the air. He winces with pain as the skin on his burnt hand stretches. He begins to play the incomplete piece from Sequence Five. The music runs out at the same point as before. Pause. LUKE's DAD appears. He joins LUKE at the piano. He plays three notes. LUKE uses these three notes to take the piece beyond its normal stopping point. The music continues for a few seconds before breaking down again. Again, LUKE's DAD provides a new direction for the music, playing three more notes for LUKE to use. It is as if LUKE's DAD is both a part of him and separate from him. He stimulates LUKE's imagination, and yet at the same time he is LUKE's imagination.

*

Outside LUKE's house. MRS LITTLE is standing in the road. She looks somehow older and more frail than before. LUKE stands opposite her.

MRS LITTLE: The police called yesterday. I'd been expecting them.

LUKE: I didn't tell them anything. About you and Barley.

MRS LITTLE: It wasn't about that. They came to see me about you. One of your friends, Jason /

LUKE: I told you, he's not my friend.

MRS LITTLE: Well, that's good, because it seems he's on his way to an institute for young offenders. He told the police you broke into my house to steal a jewellery box.

LUKE: And what did you say?

MRS LITTLE: I said you'd come to my house to play the piano a few times, but that I was certain you never had any intention to steal from me. A lie, of course. You stole a bracelet. You also read a private letter.

LUKE: Sorry.

MRS LITTLE: A letter you had no right to read.

LUKE: So why didn't you give me away?

MRS LITTLE: Because you didn't give me away. (*Pause.*) All I ever wanted, apart from Bill, was a child. When I opened that letter, those dreams died. I knew I'd never love another man, and what man would love me?

LUKE: Bill loved you.

MRS LITTLE: Bill was different. (*Pause.*) Not everything I said was a lie.

LUKE: So what really happened?

MRS LITTLE: I was driving back from my brother's funeral and I saw her in a ditch. She was bleeding from the head. She'd

74

been hit by a car. I was driving her to a phone box to call for an ambulance…and she reached out a hand to me. And it was like meeting our child, the child Bill and I never had.

LUKE: But she wasn't yours.

LITTLE: I know that. I felt guilty. But I felt…I feel…like I was meant to find her.

LUKE: But not to keep her. What about her parents?

MRS LITTLE: They let her go.

LUKE: They took their eyes off her for two seconds.

MRS LITTLE: If they can't take proper care of her /

LUKE: That's rubbish and you know it.

Pause.

MRS LITTLE: I should have got her back to them. I know that. But she seemed happy at first. Who knows, if she'd never heard the piano, she might have stayed that way. (*Pause.*) What I did was wrong. (*Pause.*) You asked me once why I keep a piano if I don't play. Bill used to play. I keep it for Bill.

Pause.

LUKE: I'm playing a concert tonight. At the village hall. I think you should come.

MRS LITTLE: I don't think so.

MRS LITTLE walks away.

SEQUENCE TWENTY

LUKE and MIRANDA play the last minute of Dance of the Blessed Spirits. As they finish, and the crowd applauds, MR HARDING steps forward…

HARDING: Ladies and gentlemen, that was Miranda Davis playing Gluck's Dance of the Blessed Spirits, accompanied by Luke Stanton on piano. Congratulations Miranda.

*More applause. LUKE walks away from the concert. MIRANDA
follows him.*

MIRANDA: Luke, where are you going?

LUKE: I need to be somewhere.

MIRANDA: What do you mean?

LUKE: The forest. I need to go back.

MIRANDA: Why?

LUKE: I don't know, I can't explain /

MIRANDA: You haven't played your piece yet.

LUKE: I'll be back in time. It's just something I've got to do, all
right?

MIRANDA: Okay.

LUKE walks away.

Luke.

LUKE: Yeah?

MIRANDA: Can I come too? I'm worried about you.

Pause.

LUKE: Yeah. I'd like that.

*

*LUKE and MIRANDA are in the forest. They arrive at the charred
oak tree.*

MIRANDA: It's your tree.

LUKE: Not my tree.

MIRANDA: I think of it as your tree.

LUKE hears a strange sound, like a musical sigh.

Luke? Are you all right?

He hears the sound again.

What's wrong?

LUKE: Nothing. But do you mind if…?

MIRANDA: You want to be on your own.

LUKE: Sorry.

MIRANDA: Don't be sorry, I understand.

LUKE: Thanks.

MIRANDA: I'll just wait over there.

LUKE: Thanks, Miranda. Are you going to be all right?

MIRANDA: Of course. Just shout if you need me.

MIRANDA goes. LUKE turns to look at the tree. He hears the noise again as his DAD appears from behind the tree. DAD smiles. LUKE slowly moves towards his DAD until their faces are almost touching. A moment of stillness and peace.

LUKE: It's okay. I'm going to be all right.

LUKE opens his arms but his DAD moves calmly away. LUKE is left alone, his arms empty, outstretched.

Dad?

Pause.

Dad?!

MIRANDA comes back.

MIRANDA: Luke? Are you all right?

He turns to see her, his arms still open. She mirrors the gesture. They hold each other and he starts to cry.

It's okay. It's okay.

LUKE: Don't let go of me.

MIRANDA: I won't. Don't let go of me.

LUKE: I won't.

They kiss, LUKE still crying. As they kiss, beautiful sound engulfs LUKE: the sound of the forest; the sound of BARLEY, MRS LITTLE, MUM, ROGER and everyone he ever met; the sound of DAD; the sound of music he has heard and music that is yet to come; the sound of 'the engine'. The kiss ends. The sounds fade, leaving only 'the engine' humming quietly.

MIRANDA: You're still crying. You're going to be okay.

LUKE: I know.

Pause.

MIRANDA: Poor thing.

LUKE: Me?

MIRANDA: The tree.

LUKE: The tree's going to be okay.

MIRANDA: Roger thinks it's going to die.

LUKE: It won't. It's singing.

MIRANDA: What?

LUKE: I can hear it singing. It's woken up.

MIRANDA smiles.

Come on, we need to get back. I'm on in ten minutes.

*

Back in the concert room. As MR HARDING addresses the audience, MRS LITTLE slips into the hall to listen.

HARDING: And now we come to the final piece of the evening, which will be played, against his doctor's wishes, by a young musician of quite exceptional talent whom it has been my pleasure and my privilege to teach in recent years. He's playing a piece of his own choosing. In fact, even I don't know what we're about to hear and the suspense is killing me. So, without further ado, it's with no small measure of pride that I give to you Luke Stanton playing a piece by…?

LUKE: Stanton.

HARDING: Stanton, and which Stanton is that?

LUKE: Both.

LUKE plays the previously unfinished piece that he composed with his DAD in Sequence Nineteen. It is brilliant and is met with ecstatic applause. End.

WWW.OBERONBOOKS.COM

Follow us on www.twitter.com/@oberonbooks
& www.facebook.com/OberonBooksLondon

Printed in the USA
CPSIA information can be obtained
at www.ICGtesting.com
LVHW020959171024
794056LV00004B/1242